THE

WATCHMAN
ON THE WALL

THE WATCHMAN ON THE WALL

Intercession

by

Dr. R. Brian Kisner

Publisher's Cataloging-in-Publication Data
Kisner, R. Brian
The Watchman on the Wall. Intercession.;
by Dr. R. Brian Kisner.
72 pages cm.
ISBN: 978-1-7373206-0-9 paperback
        978-1-7373206-1-6 ebook
1. Prayer. 2. Petition. 3. God's provision.
I. Title
2021910987

He calls out like a lion. My Lord, I stand on the watchtower all day long, I stay at my post all night.

Isaiah 21:8 CJB

TABLE OF CONTENTS

Introduction

A Fresh Perception of Intercession and an Intercessor

My intention in writing this book is not to discredit anyone who has engaged in a life of prayer and supplication. Everyone lives and dies through their own merit of who they are and what they have done for the Lord while on this earth.

Tombstones contain the beginning and ending dates of a person's life, with a dash in-between. What matters in reality is what the dash represents; whether the life encompassed by those dates was lived in fullness or wasted; whether the person so commemorated came to a relationship with Jesus early enough to grow and make a difference for the Kingdom of God, or wandered around constantly trying to find the will of God rather than living the will of God. Righteousness comes from union with Christ. But in a practical sense, righteousness must be pursued; it must be desired and attained. Prayer is the beginning of that pursuit.

Prayer is one of the prominent themes of the Bible. For this reason alone we should pay attention because we must be people of prayer. Jesus taught His disciples (and us) to pray to the Father, and Paul gave further instruction later in the New

Testament. In the Bible, when believers prayed, things happened. Lives were changed. God came and met with them and blessed them.

Supplication (also known as petitioning) is the most common form of prayer, wherein some-one makes a personal request for a provision from God. A prayer of supplication on behalf of someone else is known as intercession. In the fullest sense, however, intercession involves much more than simple supplication. Intercession is prayer for what is to come in your life and the lives of others.

When intercessors pray they are asking God for mercy, judgments, blessings, grace, healing, prosperity, and many other things. A phrase used often in Christianity to refer to intercessory prayer is, "standing in the gap," which is based on Ezekiel 22:30, "So I sought for a man among them who would make a wall, and stand in the gap before Me on behalf of the land, that I should not de-stroy it; but I found no one." I am not sure there are many saints who have done such a thing.

In this short book I want to explore the differ-ence between prayer, intercession, and the call to be an intercessor. My prayer is that you will find a place of solace in God and in prayer and be able to enhance what you already know. My desire is not to change you but to grow you into the King-dom, to water the seed that is called by your name so you can see it grow and flourish.

Chapter One

Honor: The Protocol of God's Throne Room

Honor and majesty are before Him; Strength and beauty are in His sanctuary (Psalm 96:6).

To execute on them the written judgment—This honor have all His saints. Praise the LORD! (Psalm 149:9)

I am well aware that some of you reading this book live in America. America has always been a nation of honor, yet many Americans seem to have forgotten the meaning of the word. They seem to have little or no understanding of how to show honor. I recently watched a man participate in a service to honor a soldier. Although he was a person of recognized political influence, in the presence of many military leaders and military men and women, he was like a fish out of water. His posture, decorum, and overall mannerisms betrayed his ignorance of honor and its meaning.

As children of God, we bear the "honor of God," which He has placed upon us Himself. We can define honor as respect, glory, distinction, recognition, merit and prestige. Since we have all of these things in His name, how should the "honor of God" affect the way we think about ourselves and the way we live our lives? How should it change us in order better to serve the Kingdom of God? Most importantly, how should it affect the attitude and demeanor with which we approach God? The church at large today has developed a "Papa" syndrome, where, in our diligent attempts to relate to our Father, we tend to forget that He is the Creator of the universe and everything in it. Our loving heavenly Father is also His Majesty on High, the Supreme Ruler of all. We know these things, but do we live them out in His presence?

In human societies on earth, accessibility to royalty, heads of state, or other people of power and influence is protected by rules of protocol. Protocol gives direction on the proper way to approach, address, and leave the presence of such people in order to ensure that proper honor is afforded to them because of their position. What is the protocol for entering the throne room of God? Is there such a protocol? What do the scriptures teach us to do if we are people of honor?

Enter into His gates with thanksgiving, And into His courts with praise. Be thankful to Him, and bless His name (Psalm 100:4).

Let us therefore come boldly to the throne of grace, that we may obtain mercy and find grace to help in time of need (Hebrews 4:16).

Now to Him who is able to keep you from stumbling, And to present you faultless Before the presence of His glory with exceeding joy (Jude 1:24).

I am not against any teaching about "Papa God." However, it is important to understand that there are times when you are with your Father and He is in chambers, not on the throne. These are the times when you can just kick back and enjoy the feast of God. We are to love His presence as individuals, not asking Him to judge situations, but simply loving God for who He is. When these times come, they are personal, powerful and for our edification. This is when God honors you for who you are. These are the best of times, entering His rest and celebrating life with Him.

My favorite moments are when I am standing before God in His throne room and am required to respond to Him in prayer. Don't worry if you have not yet experienced what I am talking about. We will dig a little deeper into the courtroom of God in a later chapter. For now, it is important to understand that we must honor God IN His presence. It does not matter whether you bow your head, kneel, lie prostrate, walk around, or sit in a chair. What matters is that you acknowledge that you are not the wisest or most knowledgeable person in the room and that you need to listen as well as speak. Proper protocol before God's throne requires respect for the One in whose presence you stand. This means never turning your back on Him and always speaking to Him face-to-face.

Scripture commands all of us as children of God to boldly enter His throne room of grace, not nervous or whimpering but with full understanding of who we are in Christ. Entering His courts with praise for who He is and for what He has done creates in us the proper attitude of mind for approaching His Majesty, enabling us to speak and be spoken to with reverence and confidence.

Proper protocol for approaching God focuses on humility. Humility does not mean looking down on yourself or disparaging your self-respect, but rather being submissive to God's Word and Spirit in your life. Only true humility can take place in the presence of God. True humility is heartfelt and manifests itself in a true change in your spirit. Proverbs 1:7 says that the fear of the Lord is the beginning of knowledge. It is the starting place. Going humbly and reverently to God's throne of grace and speaking respectfully to Him on behalf of someone else as Abraham did concerning Lot will bring you to a right place before God. Once you fully realize that you not only have come before God in prayer but that God is actually listening to what you are saying—once the fear of the Lord and honor begin to manifest in your spiritual walk—your prayers will change, your language will change; your whole approach will change. So let us continue to honor God and one another in all we do. Let us boldly enter into the throne room of God.

Chapter Two

The Kingdom of God is Within You

After this manner therefore pray ye: Our Father which art in heaven, Hallowed be thy name. Thy kingdom come. Thy will be done in earth, as it is in heaven. Give us this day our daily bread. And forgive us our debts, as we forgive our debtors. And lead us not into temptation, but deliver us from evil: For thine is the kingdom, and the power, and the glory, forever. Amen (Mattew 6: 9-13 KJV).

Let me make it clear that I am not trying to change your theology or your previous mindset regarding Christianity, but merely relating my own personal experiences with my heavenly Father. I want to urge you to do the same. Hold on to what you feel is sacred, and continually build on that experience. But make sure that you ground your experience in scriptural truth. To this day I adhere to something I read years ago in the preface of Watchman Nee's book, *The Spiritual Man*. If this book you are reading, or any other book, changes your perspective of God on the sole basis of self-introspection without scriptural grounding, you will not receive proper enlightenment or direction for being led into the purposes of God. The Bible is God's inerrant Word, and the secret to our creativity and purpose is found within its pages. What I wish to show you can be found in the simplicity of the scriptures. My purpose is to enlighten scripture, not change its meaning. I have no desire to show or create any thing from the scriptures that does not exist there.

While praying and meditating on the Lord one night, His presence suddenly became so sweet in the room. It was the middle of the night, quiet, and a beautiful place of peace and serenity. I began to meditate on the Lord's Prayer from Matthew chapter 6, and I began to see a deeper picture of its meaning. I began to realize that scriptures that I had been taught referred to a future time are actually relevant now. The Kingdom of God had come and was dwelling within us right now. We are no longer waiting on the Kingdom; we are in the Kingdom NOW. God's will is the Kingdom and His presence is within us and upon us.

Neither shall they say, Lo here! Or, lo there! for, behold, the kingdom of God is within you (Luke 17:21 KJV).

Thy kingdom come. Thy will be done in earth, as it is in heaven (Matthew 6:10 KJV).

I know there are those who are waiting on the Kingdom of God to come, but if that is the case, they cannot pray this prayer. Heaven and earth both are in the Kingdom of God. We must enlarge our picture of Jesus Christ to see Him alive in heaven as well as on earth, fulfilling the will of

His Father in us and through us. I understand that we are waiting on the return of Jesus Christ and that many things will change greatly when He does return. However, I also believe that the Kingdom lives within us right now and that positive change is possible today. Why, then, is change not happening in the proportions of Jesus' promise, "greater works than these" shall we do (Jn. 14:12)? Why do we not see more prayers answered? We spend much time in prayer but often fail to see the results of our prayers. I would ask you to open your mind to hear what I have to say. Permit me to challenge your thoughts and open new insights to truth.

If the Kingdom of God is within you, then whenever we pray for His will be done in earth as it is in heaven, we are praying for what is taking place on the inside to come to the outside; to bring freshness to our lives, calmness to our souls, and to let rest become a place of meditation within us. Take a moment to look inside yourself. Does Christ live in you? Does Jesus have a place in your heart? Are you alive in Him? This is a time to become excellent where you exist, to be you, letting Christ be formed in you. "He (Jesus) is before all things, and in Him all things hold together" (Col. 1:17 NASB). All things are in Him; therefore, in His image all things are in you. The inside of us (our spirit) is bigger than what is taking place on the outside of us. We must see this taking place by faith.

7

Why are you looking to an unseen world that is hard to grasp with your imagination, when the reality is that God is manifesting inside you, challenging you in your spirit to bring change to the life you live on earth? His goal, from the inside out, is to fulfill His will in earth as it is in heaven. Could it be that your FLESH, which is part of the dust of the earth from which you came, is the earth He is talking of changing, to perform His will in you? Think of what a world-changing event we would have if we could just get what is going on inside to begin to function and fulfill on the outside! The apostle Paul describes this as, "Christ in you, the hope of glory" (Col. 1:27).

So I ask you, is heaven real inside of you? Of course it is. Is heaven a real place? Absolutely! There is a parallel Kingdom that is so real that when your flesh dies, your spirit goes to live with Jesus in heaven until He returns to the earth. In the meantime, while we are living on earth in our flesh, let us begin looking inside ourselves and allow the will of God to fulfill its purpose in coming forth to the outside. Let's let His will be done in earth (in our flesh) as it is in heaven.

As we close this chapter, let's take a moment to look at some familiar scriptures. Remember that you are about to enter the courts of the Almighty God, who lives within you, so you will want to stop, prepare yourself through praise and worship, and boldly enter into His presence within you. Don't look up to the unseen but deep within to the dwelling place of the Lord. Do you know that I cannot come into the secret place God has prepared for ONLY YOU TO ENTER INTO? Your spirit is filled with His Spirit. Go, my friend, and take a moment to enjoy the righteousness, peace, and joy of the Holy Spirit, for this is the Kingdom of God within you. Enjoy!

He that dwelleth in the secret place of the most High shall abide under the shadow of the Almighty. I will say of the LORD, He is my refuge and my fortress: my God; in him will I trust (Psalm 91:1-2 KJV).

For the kingdom of God is not meat and drink; but righteousness, and peace, and joy in the Holy Ghost (Romans 14:17 KJV).

According as his divine power hath given unto us all things that pertain unto life and godliness, through the knowledge of him that hath called us to glory and virtue: (2Peter 1:3 KJV)

I trust you have taken a moment to experience the presence of God. Remember, do not lose track of your roots (where you came from) because your fruit is in your roots (Rom. 15:12). Follow my thought process here: all we are doing is entering the throne room of God. Never give up your basic faith to take on a new faith. You are like a growing tree. You are on a journey to make you who you are in Christ. My goal is to add to that process, not take away from what God has done in you up to this time in your life. The goal is not to change you but to grow you in your faith and understanding.

Finally, reread the Lord's prayer from Matthew 6:9-13. I want you to see that this prayer is about everyday living, the internal or physical issues of spirit, soul, and flesh. It has nothing to do with worldly problems, but speaks of everyday living here on earth.

Chapter Three

The Courts of God and His Chambers

Let us now discuss the difference between the courts of God and His chambers.

Draw me, we will run after thee: the king hath brought me into his chambers: we will be glad and rejoice in thee, we will remember thy love more than wine: the upright love thee (Song of Solomon 1:4 KJV).

"Draw me after you and let us run together! The king has brought me into his chambers." "We will rejoice in you and be glad; we will extol your love more than wine. Rightly do they love you" (Song of Solomon 1:4 NASB).

"Chambers" in this context refers to the innermost parts of our heart and soul. We are not simple beings, but complex. People have studied human anatomy for centuries through the discourse of spirit, soul, and body. Preachers have taught us that man is a spirit with a soul that lives in a body, and scripture shows us that this is true. We can take scripture and study about each area separately and learn how to function in each of them, but real life must include all three functioning in a divine order. That is what makes us powerful upon the earth.

There are times that we meet God in His courts, standing before the King of Kings and functioning before Him in prayer and intercession, making supplication before the Lord. We deal with praying for one another, discussing one another, crying out for mercy for one another, and taking the issues of world leaders and countries before the Lord. We discuss with Him about business and establishing righteousness in the earth, and seek His heart about the issues of life to help one another and lift one another up.

Then there are times we go before the Lord into His chambers where He invites us to enter into His rest and sit down with Him. These are quiet times in the Lord. These are times when we come to such a place of rest that we fall asleep before Him and feel thoroughly rested when we awake because we know in our hearts that this rest is different than mere physical rest. We know in our hearts that we have had a moment of serenity and honor placed upon us; our minds are focused and our flesh is vibrant with freshness. We know that something supernatural has happened in those moments and we cannot duplicate them because we did not initiate them on our own. The coming together of God and man in prayer is what brings the supernatural to the natural.

For as the heavens are higher than the earth, so are my ways higher than your ways, and my thoughts than your thoughts (Isaiah 55:9 KJV).

He made known his ways unto Moses, his acts unto the children of Israel (Ps. 103:7 KJV).

Moses was one whom God permitted to stand and wait before Him. Moses was familiar with both the throne room and the chambers. In the throne room we know the acts of God, but in the chambers we learn the ways of God. Moses was privileged to hear the Lord and to be taught His ways. Israel knew only of the acts of God; they knew the Law and the judgements. They could tell of what God had done but could not explain His reasoning and reckoning, nor His plan. Moses knew God's plan, however, because God had shared His mind and purpose with him. Moses' time at the burning bush and later on Mount Sinai gave us the written Law and the history known as the Pentatauch, the first five books of the Bible.

Our great privilege as believers is to have God's laws written on our hearts, His wisdom to speak the truth, and the enlightenment of His indwelling Spirit to perceive with accuracy the move and purpose of God. What excuse do we have not to recognize these things? What excuses do we make when we fail to do so? What things are we waiting for man to fulfill that God cannot come and breathe upon to make us move? All of these areas require a person of God to seek His face in a life of meditation and prayer, a deep desire to come into His presence and stand in the throne room or enter into His chambers. Wherever God chooses to meet us, whether in chambers or courts, is His decision. Our part is to be prepared for both.

Jesus stood in the garden one night in Gethsemane, while judgment was rendered before the throne of God in the Supreme Court of God. Remember, this is a one-time event of God in the flesh standing before God the Father and God the Spirit in judgment. The disciples only knew one way to enter into His presence, and that was into His chambers. They had just been there for supper with the Lord, and they had lain back and rested. Little did they understand that they were going from chambers to court, so they did what they knew to do: rest, relax, and let God work it out. All of us look at what they missed when they could have been standing alongside witnessing one of the greatest events of the universe. Jesus did not condemn them when He spoke to them as they slept and said, "So, you men could not keep watch with Me for one hour? Keep watching and praying that you may not enter into temptation; the spirit is willing, but the flesh is weak" (Mt. 26:40b-41 NASB).

I think there is a lesson here, that if we learn it, Jesus will not have to repeat that statement through the millennia of time, but can say instead, "Come boldly to the throne of grace." We need to understand that Jesus is looking for someone to stand with Him and intercede with Him in the courts of God where the throne of judgment and justice exists. In the throne room of God we are crying out for the burdened, bruised, and beaten; we are there to proclaim the acceptable year of the Lord. You should desire to be in a position where He can hand you the responsibility of intercession and know that you will not forsake the Kingdom. Intercession is sometimes when you know those you are praying for are wrong and have done wrong, but through intercession you seek mercy and grace on their behalf.

We must let the Christ within us take us where no man can: to the throne. *This brings a whole new meaning to boldly approaching the throne of grace.* We begin to experience what God spoke of Abraham concerning Lot in Genesis 18:17-18 (NASB): "The LORD said, 'Shall I hide from Abraham what I am about to do, since Abraham will surely become a great and mighty nation, and in him all the nations of the earth will be blessed?'" We must begin to comprehend that God does nothing on earth without discussing or making known to His servants what He is doing. Actually, He now does nothing in heaven without including us. He desires that we be a part of Creation and speak into what is going on. Men are now speaking throughout the earth of what God is showing them that is taking place in heaven. God is also speaking to those on earth who will listen to what He is doing on earth.

My prayer times permit me to know areas God is working in the lives of people, but it is not my place to discuss those things with them. I pray for them and watch the hand of God move on their behalf. I find great joy in watching God touch lives and for those who are touched to come alive in knowing that it was the Lord's doing. Some of my best intercession time is when the Lord and I rejoice over what He has done.

Chapter Four

Interceding in the Throne Room

Intercession is inseparably connected to one of the high positions held by Jesus Christ as He is seated even now at the right hand of His Father in heaven. He is our Advocate, the Intercessor for mankind. As our Advocate and Intercessor, Jesus chose to bear a cross and become the Redeemer of all mankind. I continually keep in mind this thought, which, although it is not scripture, is nevertheless true: *Jesus went somewhere I could not go myself and did for me something I could not do for myself.* Jesus acted as my Intercessor (and yours) at the time of the cross and still is acting as Intercessor today. You and I are eternally attached to His intercession. Jesus stands as our Advocate, but to understand this, we must delve deeper into the meaning of "advocate."

> *My little children, these things write I unto you, so that you may not sin. And if anyone sins, we have an Advocate with the Father, Jesus Christ the righteous* (1 John 2:1).

Princeton WordNet defines advocate (noun) as a proponent or exponent, a person who pleads for a cause or propounds an idea. As a verb that means counsel, counselor, or pleader, as in a lawyer who pleads a case in court. To advocate means to recommend, to urge, to push for something; to speak, to preach, or to argue in favor of something or someone.

These definitions should give us a better idea of what Jesus does for us continually from His throne as our Advocate/Intercessor. A more common word for advocate in today's language is "attorney," but I will stick with the word advocate to help imbed in your mind what Jesus does for us.

I want to create a scenario, a picture, of what this might possibly look like, with the understanding that the reality is certainly much deeper and richer and more beautiful than any picture we could paint. When we are finished looking at the work of an intercessor from this viewpoint, I would strongly urge you to ask the Holy Spirit to build within your spirit an understanding of the reality of how an intercessor/advocate stands in the presence of God.

The throne room is also a court room. It is not a magistrate's office; you must think higher than that. You must think bigger, like the Supreme Court or the World Court, a place of Majestic authority, a place full of judgment, grace, and mercy with the fullness of goodness and the Shekinah glory of God there. Jesus is there; the room is full of His Spirit. Love abounds in this courtroom, and the only fear present is a reverential fear of the Lord. In this place absolute truth prevails; dissention and confusion are exposed and removed. Righteousness in the divine Courtroom is unmistakably evident, righteousness of a depth and purity that can be neither comprehended nor explained by human earthly experience. This absolute Righteousness is the only reason you have access to God's throne room, because it is Jesus' life work.

Close your eyes now and imagine yourself walking into that throne/courtroom. You are not trembling, weak, or scared; on the contrary, you are confident – BOLD. You are given a seat where you can speak and be spoken to equally. Above all else, you are *heard* as a representative of the Kingdom of God. Now you are positioned to be an intercessor, to take your place before the throne of grace and speak on behalf of those whom He has placed on your heart. Now you are a member of the advocate force of God in the earth. You have the right to transcend in the Spirit, to avail yourself in prayer and supplication.

Intercession is a high and holy calling. It is not my goal to scare you out of prayer but for you to be able to rightly divide the Word of Truth and stand where you are called to stand. We need not shrink back from responsibility but press into the high calling that is set before us.

The fear of the LORD is the beginning of wisdom; A good understanding have all those who do His commandments. His praise endures forever (Psalm 111:10).

The fear of the LORD is the beginning of knowledge, But fools despise wisdom and instruction (Proverbs 1:7).

We must learn to stand as Abraham stood when he interceded for Lot's family and to have the boldness that Abraham had as he spoke concerning Lot and his family. We also need to make a decision with absolute wisdom as seen in the writings of King Solomon in the book of Proverbs. We must not forget God's words to Jeremiah when He called the prophet to proclaim his allegiance to God and take a stand against the Babylonians:

But the Lord said to me, "Do not say, 'I am a youth,' Because everywhere I send you, you shall go, and all that I command you, you shall speak. Do not be afraid of them, For I am with you to deliver you," declares the LORD (Jeremiah1:7-8).

Remember that no one believed in Jeremiah, let alone believed with him. We have not been called to intercede only for those who are well but also for those who have fallen into sin and those who are sick and need healing. We need to be people who will stand in the face of adversity for others, not condemning them, even though they are in that position, but leading them into the courts of grace and mercy. We need also to stand before a living God on their behalf and cry out for what is theirs through the covenant of God: that which is blood-bought (set free through the shedding of

Jesus' blood) and has been redeemed (price paid for sins and shortcomings) through Jesus Christ.

I do not care where your doctrinal knowledge in Christianity takes you or what you have become, the entrance into the throne of grace is and will always be through that which was done in Jesus' flesh upon that cross and the sprinkling of the blood of the Lamb on the mercy seat of heaven. "Therefore let us draw near with confidence to the throne of grace, so that we may receive mercy and find grace to help in time of need"(Heb. 4:16 NASB). Without that, you have nothing.

That is your defense: the right and ability to enter the throne room, come into the presence of your Father, and make your petitions known. That is where your power lies. It is your right as a child of God to acknowledge and express your heart and mind before Him and to stand and pray in His presence. In His presence you find your calling, and in that calling you are welcomed and permitted to express yourself. You first must be able to acknowledge that you are welcome and then be open to be a part of what is about to be spoken to you. This is the beginning of intercession for someone is called to be an intercessor. This is where you will be most effective in your Christian walk with your relationship to your Father and to the body of Christ. The blood of Jesus is where you intercede from. His blood has been sprinkled on the mercy seat of heaven, and there in His presence you are permitted to speak and learn to listen. Upon entering the throne room you will find an atmosphere of rest; enter into it. Hebrews 4:11 tells us to "be diligent to enter that rest, so that no one will fall" (NASB). We must come into God's atmosphere, where He breathes life and lives. Acts 17:28 says, "For in him we live, and move, and have our being: as certain also of your own poets have said, For we are also his offspring" (KJV).

The blood of Jesus will now have a deep expression in your life. This is where you will intercede from: the throne, the mercy seat, and the blood of Jesus. Know this one thing: you are welcomed into this place.

Chapter Five

Transcending to the Third Heaven

I cannot go any further without taking a moment to explain that there are various heavens. Most faiths teach that there are three heavens. The first heaven is where we live and function. The second heaven is a spiritual realm: "For we do not wrestle against flesh and blood, but against the rulers, against the authorities, against the cosmic powers over this present darkness, against the spiritual forces of evil in the heavenly places" (Eph. 6:12 ESV). The second heaven is where we must engage in spiritual warfare to overcome and achieve breakthrough. Spiritual warfare, however, is only part of what intercession is. The third heaven is where the Father resides and sits on His throne. This heaven is the place we talk about where the saints go who pass on. Genesis 1:1 teaches us that God created the heavens and the earth. Paul wrote of this third heaven,

I know a man in Christ who fourteen years ago— whether in the body I do not know, or whether out of the body I do not know, God knows—such a one was caught up to the third heaven (2 Corinthians 12:2).

As Christians we must understand that we have the right to transcend to all three heavens. We live here in the first, we battle in the second, and we visit in the third. I also want to say that what I am talking about is not for the fainthearted. I trust you are not reading this book just to find a way to become spiritually 'weird.' I am talking about becoming aware of the times where being able to walk into the presence of God when He calls is necessary. Remember the call to boldness in Hebrews: "Let us therefore come boldly to the throne of grace, that we may obtain mercy and find grace to help in time of need" (Heb. 4:16).

I believe that this is not just a place of prayer and "feeling good," but a literal place that you can go (if permitted) and rest in the audience of His Majesty. I find there are many people who talk the talk but do not walk the walk. You do not enter into some of these areas without the fear of the Lord upon you. There are times when the situation is so intense or things happen that I hesitate in His presence, out of nothing other than sheer reverence, when I feel more fully the presence of God and realize who He truly is: all-majesty, and there is nothing small or ordinary about Him. Having had the privilege of being in His presence, I am humbled and full of honor that I have been permitted to stand before Him.

Intercessors have the God-given right to come into His presence and function in His courts, but reverence and respect must be seen in our lives before we can enter into these places.

To speak boldly is to speak freely, frankly, openly, unreserved and without concealment. It means to speak without ambiguity or circumlocution and without the use of figures and comparisons. In deportment, to be bold means to express free and fearless confidence, cheerful courage, and assurance.

Do you realize that in the presence of God nothing is concealed? Everything is out on the table for inspection. God brings you into a place to talk and intercede knowing more than you do about the situation. He does this because God loves righteousness and interaction with His family. He teaches us His ways and His culture; it gives Him as a Father the opportunity to express Himself before you. The Father builds our faith as we come before Him, and we learn to draw from Him the power of His being through His Word and by His Spirit. Interaction with the Father is absolute and pure.

Here is the problem: most intercessors reach the second heaven, get involved in the battle, and come back with knowledge about what darkness and the devil and evil are doing, but never ascend to the actual presence of God where the answers reside. Anybody can pray and tell someone else what the devil is planning. Palm readers can do that; tarot card readers can do that; but what they cannot do is go to the third heaven and go before the living God and cause righteousness, peace, and joy to manifest on those for whom they pray to help bring them a victory from a place of oppression and depression.

So we see that the task of the intercessor is to break through and break down the darkness to stand in the presence of God on behalf of those for whom they intercede. I tell businesspeople that I pray for that it will take me a year to completely break through and begin to understand what they do as a business and to comprehend spiritually how to fully benefit them in intercession.

Take a moment now and go before the Lord. Meditate on the scripture that He wants to share with you right now and listen to Him. Rest in Him a little and worship Him with thanksgiving. Know that He loves you enough to give you access to His throne anytime you desire to come.

Think on this:

Every time you call on the name of the Lord, there is a place for you to stand and plead your case.

Is that awesome or what?!

Chapter Six

Intercession is a Lifestyle

We know from our study of the inerrant Word of God that heaven is real and is the place where God dwells. It is also where the souls of departed saints abide while awaiting Jesus' return. We know, too, of the heavens that exist above us as we gaze in wonder at the splendor of the celestial bodies and the universe that surrounds us. Finally, we know from the Bible that the Kingdom of God is within us, as Jesus said. There is, therefore, a heaven of the heart, where the Holy Spirit dwells. Three heavens, then, and all three dwell within the Kingdom of God.

Paul described the heaven of the heart this way:

What? Know ye not that your body is the temple of the Holy Ghost which is in you, which ye have of God, and ye are not your own? For ye are bought with a price: therefore glorify God in your body, and in your spirit, which are God's (1 Corinthians 6:19-20 KJV).

We can recognize this heaven by the evidence of the Kingdom within us:

Neither shall they say, Lo here! or, Lo there! for, behold, the kingdom of God is within you (Luke 17:21 KJV).

It is vitally important that we understand that we must no longer separate in our minds God's dwelling places on earth and in heaven. We must open ourselves for God to dwell in fullness wherever He sees fit, and that is within us by the Holy Spirit, who dwells in the "temple" of our body. We are not mere flesh and bone, the dust of the earth; we are heavily beings residing in earthly bodies. The Holy Spirit resides with us, and we reflect His glory.

Arise, shine; for your light has come, And the glory of the LORD has risen upon you (Isaiah 60:1 NASB).

Our spirits are the temple of God, full of glory, full of light. You need to rise up and take your place in this light and glory. As Jesus said,

Let your light shine before men in such a way that they may see your good works, and glorify your Father who is in heaven (Matthew 5:16 NASB).

The apostle Paul described the distinct characteristics of his heart-temple:

For the kingdom of God is not meat and drink; but righteousness, and peace, and joy in the Holy Ghost (Romans 14:17 KJV).

This is the Kingdom within us, which is a part of the heavenlies. God has given us "all things that pertain to life and godliness" (2 Pet. 1:3). All we need to do is step up into it by faith, filled with the desire to walk out the faith that is in our hearts. We must open ourselves up and listen to what the Holy Spirit says to our hearts individually, and pursue the challenges that He gives us as He speaks. I believe it is important for every believer to learn to follow his or her own heart, to journal regularly, and to be aware that God treats each of His children individually in this life. The Spirit of God must touch every person's purpose and performance. When it comes to intercession, no two intercessors are alike, praying the same things over the same people. There is great diversity in the Kingdom of God, and each of us lives it out differently in our own individual expressiveness. This is the way God expands His Kingdom through prayer.

According as his divine power hath given unto us all things that pertain unto life and godliness, through the knowledge of him that hath called us to glory and virtue (2Peter 1:3 KJV).

We already have these things to live our lives for Him. God has given us the gifts, talents, and character to enable us to function in the areas to which He has called us. The Bible says that we are made to be seated in heavenly places in Christ Jesus:

And hath raised us up together, and made us sit together in heavenly places in Christ Jesus (Ephesians 2:6 KJV).

We need to recognize that God has already placed us in a position of rest; this is His desire for us. "Therefore, let us fear if, while a promise remains of entering His rest, any one of you may seem to have come short of it" (Heb. 4:1 NASB). He encourages us to come into this place of rest and have fellowship with Him. Together we are to develop an atmosphere of rest and comfort. Jesus said, "Take My yoke upon you and learn from Me, for I am gentle and humble in heart, and YOU WILL FIND REST FOR YOUR SOULS" (Mt. 11:29 NASB).

We are made to sit together. I remember when I was a child, my father would call a family meeting and make us all come and sit with one another. We would get quiet because we knew either that we were in trouble or that he had decided that we all needed some family time together. Sometimes he gave us instruction, or talked to us about the things of life, or laid out the chores we each would be responsible for because his work schedule was changing again. He wanted to ensure that the necessary tasks at home were taken care of while he was on his shifts at the steel mill. Whatever it was, it was a time when he had our full attention for the moment and we were attentive and ready to listen. Looking back, I am amazed at how many times we got together and rather than listen to what was being spoken, we were busy chattering with each other, trying to tell our story, or a better story, or give input to help us feel as though we were taking part in the conversation so we did not feel inferior. I want to encourage you not to be surprised if, as you read this book, you find that you have input that expands on what I am saying. All that means is that I have one part of the picture and you have another part. As we fit the parts together, we will see the bigger picture.

Intercessors are a vital part of the body of Christ and of what God is doing on the earth, but intercessors do not have the full revelation of God. We must remember that intercession is not a gift but a lifestyle; it is what you are meant to do with your life, and what you have been separated to do and bring back to the Kingdom.

Intercession is not worship and praise. It is not preaching and prophecy, or one of the five-fold gifts, nor any other gift within itself. Intercession utilizes all the gifts to get the job done. You can flow in and out of various giftings as you intercede, but intercession itself is not a gift; it is a calling. There is a lot of difference between gifting and calling.

The ability to transcend the heavenlies to the throne of God is a calling. God calls you to His throne, but how you function in the calling is your gifting. "But when God, who set me apart even from my mother's womb and called me through His grace...(Gal. 1:15 NASB) First, there is the *eternal* call of grace. There must be an advanced call from God on your life. You cannot make yourself an intercessor. Second, there is the *effectual* call of grace The eternal call becomes the effectual call when we submit to the Holy Spirit to become an intercessor. Such a one will have a divine commission behind him, a divine summons before him, and a divine conviction within him.

Choosing to walk in the call of God as an intercessor takes you into the spirit realm that makes you useful to fulfill the will of God. God desires those He can share His heart with in certain situations, and those who will cry out on behalf of others to see transition take place in those for whom they intercede. Intercession can be taught, but only by the Holy Spirit. Most important of all, intercession must be experienced.

There is a throne in your heart where you walk with God on a daily basis, but there is also a throne of God that administers judgments and righteousness. There is a place that transcends the mortality of man and his ability to get to God; you must experience this in the Spirit of God. In prayer, the throne room of God and the throne room of your heart become one; there is no separation. You must walk in the Spirit of God and seek His Kingdom and His righteousness. This is a place where we walk not in the natural, but the supernatural—a place I like to call "Highway 35" (Isaiah 35). It is a holy place where you do not experience fear.

A highway shall be there, and a road, And it shall be called the Highway of Holiness. The unclean shall not pass over it, But it shall be for others. Whoever walks the road, although a fool, Shall not go astray. No lion shall be there, Nor shall any ravenous beast go up on it; It shall not be found there. But the redeemed shall walk there, And the ransomed of the-Lord shall return, And come to Zion with singing, With everlasting joy on their heads. They shall obtain joy and gladness, And sorrow and sighing shall flee away (Isaiah 35:8-10).

This place, I believe, is obtainable from this side of heaven. We have placed so much spiritual awareness on the afterlife, that we often forget what is available to us this side of heaven. Jesus came back from the dead. He is risen. Therefore, everything we do is now from the position that we are born again into the Kingdom, and it is from an eternal position that we function. Jesus is the Chief Intercessor. He was resurrected, He is alive, and is in intercession for us, making it possible for us to obtain the things spoken of in the new covenant. As I said before, we now have all things that pertain to life and godliness: "seeing that His divine power has granted to us everything that pertains to life and godliness, through the true knowledge of Him who called us by His own glory and excellence" (2 Pe. 1:3 NASB).

We have an entrance into the presence of God to fulfill the will of God. Some do not believe that we live in a time of the Kingdom. I say, "Arise and shine! For the Light is come!" How can you pray for the sick and not believe that it is God's will to heal? If you believe for healing, then you must believe it is the will of God. And if you believe it is the will of God, then you must believe that the Kingdom has come and that His will is being done here on earth.

I am so excited to be part of what is going on! You must renew your mind by building your faith in Him, casting down any imaginations or anything that exalts itself against God. God must rule our hearts; we must seek Him and be found in Him. The place we seek in Him becomes our personal garden experience. God must find us clothed in righteousness, not self-justification. When the Lord comes, we must be ready, not hiding, where He has to seek us out. Isaiah said, "Here am I Lord," so we should say the same. I want to encourage you to take a few minutes to go before the Lord and offer yourself to Him by saying, "Here am I, Lord, send me."

Then I heard the voice of the Lord, saying, "Whom shall I send, and who will go for Us?" Then I said, "Here am I. Send me!" (Isaiah 6:8 NASB)

Chapter Seven

Planting Prayer Seeds

Now that we have the groundwork in place, it is time to plant some seeds. Prayer = *communication*. When I want to communicate with another person, I may talk or write, but I do not pray. Prayer is different from merely "talking" to God. Prayer has been defined as communication with God, but let's break that down a bit more as there are other terms we must understand that can also be considered communication with God. For example, there is petition, supplication, intercession and thanksgiving.

> *Confess your faults one to another, and pray one for another, that ye may be healed. The effectual fervent prayer of a righteous man availeth much* (James 5:16 KJV).

The Message paraphrase has a rendering of this verse that I love:

> *Make this your common practice: Confess your sins to each other and pray for each other so that you can live together whole and healed. The prayer of a person living right with God is something powerful to be reckoned with* (James 5:16 MESSAGE).

> *Therefore I exhort first of all that supplications, prayers, intercessions, and giving of thanks be made*

for all men, for kings and all who are in authority, that we may lead a quiet and peaceable life in all godliness and reverence. For this is good and acceptable in the sight of God our Savior (1 Timothy 2:1-3).

The word "petition" is used mostly in the Old Testament. First John 5:15 contains the word "petitions," the only time the word appears in the entire New Testament. This verse says that if we make our request know to God, we can know that we have the *petitions* we have asked of Him. So in the New Testament, petitioning relates to prayer. It is non-specific, asking God the simple questions of life and constantly looking to hear and see the workings of the Lord.

Supplications are prayers for healing, the offering of an olive branch of peace, etc. They are requests that totally rely on God's movement and provision. I believe this is why the Bible tells us to watch with all perseverance.

Praying always with all prayer and supplication in the Spirit, and watching thereunto with all perseverance and supplication for all saints (Ephesians 6:18 KJV).

Be anxious for nothing, but in everything by prayer and supplication, with thanksgiving, let your requests be made known to God (Philippians 4:6).

There is a slight difference between supplication and intercession. It is a fine line, but there is a difference. I believe we actually follow it unknowingly, but making the distinction is important.

Supplication is more advisory prayer (i.e. the Olive Branch), as we pray for the President and the government, for example. Although there are some specific areas of prayer we can bring before God in intercession, the basic type of praying that we do is to make supplication. We ask God to intervene because we do not know the hearts of those involved or the details of their situation. Rarely does the public know much at all about the complexity of the workings of government and the specific details of the overall situation. I do not personally know the President of the United States of America, but I pray for him. I offer up supplications for him, asking God to speak to him and intervene in his life. I must believe that God knows him more than I do, and therefore, because I do not know him personally, I don't have the necessary communication with him to know the specifics with which to intercede on his behalf. I can only intercede for what I know specifically, and must make supplications for the rest. I cannot properly represent the President before the throne of God as an advocate, but I can make supplication to the Chief Intercessor, Jesus, to speak and move on his behalf.

To make the prayers of supplication real to us I want to use once again the courtroom scenario.

When two attorneys are handling a case together, they have different roles they play to contribute to the task. The lead attorney takes the main role and is involved in the many details of the case, whereas the secondary attorney manages the overall picture. The secondary attorney has responsibility to listen, grasp the bigger picture, and offer advice and encouragement to the defense or lead attorney. This is the position of supplication; it is a secondary position. I have the power in supplication to speak to the intercessor or primary defense and encourage or advise from my position.

I want you to see the power of supplication. God is asking you to counsel, advise, and encourage the Chief Intercessor to speak properly on behalf of the person he is representing. Think of Jesus as the Chief Intercessor, and you are there in supplication, representing the person in the courts of heaven. You have become co-counsel to the throne of God on their behalf, and the primary counsel is Jesus!!! Jesus and you become the defense team that is pleading the case before the Father. There is no end to what we can accomplish in prayer.

If you are saying, "Wow! Does this really work?" I would like to invite you to try it for yourself. Think of something that is on your heart, that you have prayed for fervently, but you do not have all the facts or information necessary to pray properly. Jesus knows all of the missing information you do not have, so begin by asking Jesus to give proper representation to the situation. Encourage God to use His wisdom and reveal the truth of the matter. Although the statement might sound reversed in its meaning, encouraging God takes place in worship and prayer. To have someone take the time and be devoted to being with you and becoming friends with you is not a one-sided thing on God's part. Jesus did all He did so that we might be family, and family members communicate with one another. This involves not just parents to children, but children to parents. As a grandfather, I love it when my grandsons come and sit with me and ask questions and seek wisdom. This is fulfilling, and when we come to God, because He is a rewarder of those who diligently seek Him, He is encouraged. So today take a moment and encourage God for who He is. He loves it. Spend some time with the Lord and then we will move on to look more into intercession.

When Peter was in prison (Acts Chapter 12) and no one knew the outcome, the church prayed for intervention, and Jesus sent angels to deliver him. When Peter showed up at the door, those who had been praying for him were surprised. They had not been interceding for Peter because they lacked knowledge of the specific situation. All they knew was that Peter could be beaten or killed, or made a spectacle of by whipping and torture. No one knew the specifics, but with supplication, God sent the angel. Supplication is powerful. Do not underestimate what you can accomplish working alongside the Lord.

Chapter Eight

Intercession: Praying from Knowledge

We are now ready to examine intercession in greater depth. Intercession requires knowledge of specific situations, and there are only two avenues by which this knowledge can come. The first avenue is the prompting of the Holy Spirit. He comes to you and reveals what is going on and what is about to take place so that you can join Him in the ministry of intercession. In order to avoid misunderstanding, let me hasten to say that I believe that God does nothing on the earth without talking to His servants (Amos 3:7). Someone knows something, whether it is a premonition, a prophecy, an unction, a vision, or a dream. God does nothing on this earth without man knowing about it. He has nothing to hide; as the Author of all things, He knows the full plan and timeframe for that plan. God speaks to His sons about what is going on in the earth.

The second avenue by which we can receive knowledge for intercession is when someone comes to us with a specific need and a request for intercession. As an intercessor, you must know if it is a ministry, business, personal, or family situation. Someone has to tell you something in order for you to intercede for them. There must be a point of contact, a reason, a purpose, or an understanding of what you are interceding for. We cannot just pick things out of the sky and pray for them. We must have knowledge and insight into what we are praying for if we are to properly intercede.

I have sat in what we in the church world call "intercession meetings" and listened to people pray. I have watched saints begin to pray about a situation, and before they are done, rather then praying for that situation, they have expanded their mindset to include ten other areas that had no precedence or relation to where they started.

I want to use myself as a personal example. When someone meets me, it is obvious to them that I am a large man. (My doctors say that 210 pounds is a good weight for a person of my height.) Several years ago I began to gain weight and could not control it. I will confess that I am a "meat and potatoes" person and had to work to give that up. I developed other physical problems to go along with my weight, which finally peaked at 424 pounds. At times, I would eat nothing and still not lose any weight. I changed lifestyles, sought medical help, and tried numerous diets, but could not get my health in check.

Finally, I was admitted to the Veteran's Affairs hospital for eight days, suffering from infected legs with open sores. Breathing was also a problem, but I understood it was my weight pushing on my lungs, and if I lost the extra weight, I would breathe easier. Some pulmonary tests and a chest x-ray revealed that I had an oxygen transfer problem in my lungs. My sleeping habits allowed me to sleep only two hours at a time, which meant that I did not get actual refurbish time or regeneration of oxygen in the blood that is accomplished with eight hours' sleep. I was unable to rejuvenate my oxygen levels sufficiently. I agreed to go on a B-Pap machine, which helped me breathe properly so I could attain the level of sleep I needed, and began to wear it as much as possible. Within a month I was able to get my metabolism going again and began to lose weight.

What we learned was that I was praying about my weight when my problem was pulmonary. I had to learn the hard way. Once I began getting the right amount of oxygen, I lost 60 lbs. on a diet in five months. I took a small break, and as soon as I lost the discipline, I gained the weight back. I have worked with doctors for four years on the problem, and have overcome apnea and other related issues that were hindering me from returning to the path leading to proper health and restoration. The problem was that my metabolism was not working as it should due to a lack of oxygen to my body.

I continued to pray, and God spoke to me to move to Riverview, Florida. I began educational classes at the James Haley VA Center in Tampa,

FL, and continued in them, still praying for my health, for 16 months. My health continued to deteriorate and no one could locate the problem. Yet I faithfully kept all my appointments at the VA. In short, from 2009 to 2015 I made over 350 doctor, lab, and dietician visits. Eventually, it was determined that I needed surgery to correct a problem I had been born with. In the 16 months following the surgery, my weight dropped from 392 pounds to 259 pounds. From my peak of 424 pounds, I have lost 165 pounds; my ultimate weight goal is 210 lbs. That is another chapter of my life, but one that without intercession and faith (which included the doctors' visits), I would not be alive. Today I am not on any medications, take all the necessary vitamins, and have perfect blood pressure and cholesterol. I loved myself enough to cry out in intercession for myself, along with others who loved me and cried out also. I learned intercession and prayer through what I experienced. It was during this eight-year venue of my life that I learned intercession. My time spent alone with the Lord became priceless, and to this day the life-changing effect it has had on me has become part of my eternal destiny.

There are two types of knowledge on the earth: *gnosis* and *epi-gnosis*. Gnosis is earthly knowledge found in the natural sciences and in textbooks. Epi-Gnosis, in contrast, comes from the Spirit and Word of God. Gnosis means "knowledge," while epi-gnosis means "knowledge from above" or from God. Sometimes people will ask for intercession and share the knowledge from their hearts, telling you what they want you to pray about, but that is not necessarily the whole truth. It is what *they* want you to pray about. When you begin to pray, God begins to combine their knowledge with His. This is the knowledge that comes from God and fills in the full truth that needs to be prayed about. Thus the process of intercession begins by praying for what they want, not necessarily what they need. At times, I have prayed for people and God opened avenues for them, but they refused to walk in them, choosing instead to sit and wait until something appeared to be what they wanted. This is not faith, but foolishness and presumption. These folks are what I call "bratty Christians." They must have their way because they have chosen to pervert good teaching on relationship with God and hold out for their own will. They either do not know or do not care that God has a plan bigger than theirs. I have never failed to pray for someone who asked for it, but some of them have failed to walk out their destiny because of their inability to change.

Those who pray do not fail in bringing the need before God; their purpose is to be part of the answer and the fulfillment. There are times, especially during crisis, when there seems to be little more to hang onto than prayer, and when that happens, we must also build up faith. We pray in faith. Sometimes God intervenes miraculously, but not always. Sometimes He requires faith to arise.

Remember the admonition of James 516:

Confess your faults one to another, and pray one for another, that ye may be healed. The effectual fervent prayer of a righteous man availeth much (KJV).

And in the modern paraphrase:

Make this your common practice: Confess your sins to each other and pray for each other so that you can live together whole and healed. The prayer of a person living right with God is something powerful to be reckoned with (MESSAGE).

May the Lord God of your fathers make you a thousand times more numerous than you are, and bless you as He has promised you! (Deuteronomy 1:11)

I am an 'avail much' person from James 5:16. The scripture from Deuteronomy is such a wonderful promise! Just think,when I pray for businesses, I pray that they become a thousand times more than they are now. That is a huge undertaking of change for most businesses, but I believe that God has a plan for them to prosper. We must become people who look at the bigger picture in life, having visions and goals built on the Word of God and what the Spirit is speaking to us. We must be cautious, if we don't see it manifest in a short period of time, not to begin to wonder why and then try to do things to help God change His plan. I remember when my daughter Shelley was serving Mercy Ships Ministries aboard the Caribbean Mercy Hospital ship. The prevailing thought at the time was, "The main thing is to keep the main thing the main thing." Never allow yourself to become distracted from your purpose and the goals of your heart. Always remember why you began to do what you are doing and where you purpose to go.

After spending much time in prayer in 1997, I was caught up in a revival at the church I pastored in Uniontown Pennsylvania, when the Lord manifested in power and, by His Spirit, took over for twelve weeks. We stopped the revival services at twelve weeks and then looked around to see what we had accomplished. We had prayed for the Lord to expand us as a church and, of course, to draw many people into the Kingdom for His purpose. Statistics revealed that over a period of 10 weeks, 600 people had walked through the door of a church that normally had 90–100 in attendance every week. During that same period, we added only one new church member. That is when we realized that our purpose in the Kingdom was to touch lives for Christ, and that growth of our church was not as important for the purposes of God. In this case, intercession led to an open door for God to begin moving in a community and a church in a totally unexpected way.

During the revival, I met a man named Moses Simpkins, who had connections with an organization in Pittsburgh known as the Pittsburgh Leadership Foundation, which had started the Pittsburgh Community Storehouse. He invited us to come to the warehouse and be blessed by the stores that it offered to pastors in the community. We began taking a van of people there to work. Soon, we began bringing items of necessity (clothing, goods, maintenance articles) back to our church, Bread of Life Tabernacle in Fayette County, PA, to provide for the church and for the poor. This began enhancing our small outreach known as the Love Cupboard. We continued to support the Storehouse and continued to haul everything from new clothes to painting supplies and arts and crafts, to name a few, to Fayette County. Within two years, we opened the Uniontown Community Storehouse and began to affiliate with direct pickup from World Vision in their Appalachian program. We eventually purchased a warehouse in Uniontown, and for the next ten years put close to $35 million of product (from many different donors) throughout the eastern United States, Appalachia in three states, and two nations.

The influence of what the Bread of Life Tabernacle and the Uniontown Community Storehouse developed continued to grow to various outreaches known as the Love Cupboard, which was local at the church, and Gospel on Wheels, which traveled to low-income housing units throughout western Pennsylvania delivering love, goods, and the gospel. "Saturday Nite Live with Jesus" became an outreach to communities, preaching and sharing the gospel in drama and song, and delivering necessities to young and old, along with the salvation message. As the ministry grew, we touched untold tens of thousands of people with household items and office supplies. All of this was the result of intercession and of what God chose to do. Our church never grew in stature as most see churches grow, but those 100 members of Bread of Life Tabernacle, because of intercession for our community, helped build stability in our community, built relationships with 41 other organizations, and sent tractor-trailer loads of relief supplies to Hurricane Katrina victims. The stories are too many to list. We became a church that followed wherever the Lord took us in prayer. We prayed, we worked, and we fulfilled the purpose of God for that season—all because of intercession.

This is what prayer will do when you ask God to act without a mindset of your own as to what you think He should do, but allowing Him to do whatever He chooses. For 10 years we made a powerful impact in our community, county, state, and nation, plus nations abroad. We impacted schools, churches, governments, social organizations, police, fire, and hazmat operations. I was invited to be part of a rural initiative under the direction of the Health and Human Services of the U.S. Government to develop rural America. The Storehouse developed a memorandum of understanding with the Local Community Action in providing and supporting one another in our purpose and cause. We provided windows for newly-developed low-income housing. Prayer and provision made it affordable finally for low-income families to own their own homes.

All this was the plan of God that came out of prayer, with no human agenda other than to fulfill the purpose of God. Let me say it again: intercession and prayer will move aside the agenda of man and fulfill the purpose of God.

At this point I think it is appropriate to thank key people who were involved in this ten years of my transition. First, my wife Sharon, who undeniably stood by me and pushed me, rebuked me, challenged me, and waited on me as we served the Lord together. To my daughters Larissa, Shelley, and Garnett, who did without me at times so others could be with me.

Gene and Karen Strite, who planted a seed in me that I could be more than I ever anticipated or expected, believing in me and encouraging me when they had no idea where I was headed.

Larry and Chris Gipe, who just walked into my life and took pressure off me. Larry ran the Storehouse operations in Uniontown and kept order in check when trucks of donations flooded in; also for their efforts with their own ministry, Good Works and GIG Coffee House, and in developing the Transitional Home for Women.

Jim and Veronica Martin, who gave us their barn for storing toys when we had nowhere else to keep them, for taking care of Gospel on Wheels, and for operating the outreaches.

Bertha Mulik and Wilma Wilson, who faithfully kept the Love Cupboard going, sorting clothing and overseeing the used clothing area of the Storehouse.

Bob and Carol Dean, who oversaw the Gospel on Wheels, made sure the bus got to where it needed to go, and ensured the hot dogs were ready.

John and Kelley Broadwater, who developed "Saturday Nite Live with Jesus," reaching the lost and loving the poor in a special way.

And then there is Jeff Fike, who was the backbone of everything we did, my riding buddy in the truck, the master of a pallet jack. He is a son to me and I will ever be grateful for his life. Whenever we look at Jeff, it is easy to see Jesus walking amongst us.

Bread of Life Tabernacle of Uniontown, who will always be home sweet home, for all those who supported and believed in us, and even those who didn't. For those who got mad, I choose to remember your love for me and for the grace God has shown in you. For those who rejoiced, I will always remember your love. All of this was because of intercession; it grew relationships that touched lives. I never would have dreamed of what could have been accomplished. Intercession took this small church outside the box of a traditional Christian mindset. Intercession was our most powerful tool.

Chapter Nine

Find and Fill Your Place in the Kingdom

At the end of the last chapter I mentioned many of those who made a way for me to do what we did in outreach programs. There are so many that I am sure I have left some out, but rest assured that you are in my heart, and I hold all of you in deepest appreciation. Intercession is about all of those whom God has put in your heart.

I am not one who believes that God chatters all day long. He spoke the Word, and if you decide to, you could read the entire New Testament in a matter of hours. God packs a lot into a little. He trusts that He does not have to direct every step we take, and leads us by the Holy Spirit through instinct, intuition, and prompting. God can speak five words and you can function on it for your whole life. Fulfillment is a major part of faithfulness. One thing I find lacking in many Christians is fulfillment. They are never satisfied, and never come to a place of peace with their faith. Christianity is not running a marathon, and there are no goals to score, no records to break. The race we run is one with time and discipline. Intercession, even for ourselves, can help bring this satisfaction that is so necessary in our lives.

John 14:27 in the Amplified Bible reads:

Peace I leave with you; My [own] peace I now give and bequeath to you. Not as the world gives do I give to you. Do not let your hearts be troubled, neither let them be afraid. [Stop allowing yourselves to be agitated and disturbed; and do not permit yourselves to be fearful and intimidated and cowardly and unsettled.]

This scripture is so important to understanding intercession, we must become people of untroubled hearts and not be afraid of what we face.

As you travel through this life you meet many people—acquaintances, friends, loved ones, family—and they all have a purpose to help fulfill your destiny. Whether they are in your life for five minutes, five years, or fifty years, there is a reason and purpose for them entering your atmosphere. One of those reasons is intercession. Let me explain. Have you ever been looking at a beautiful view, such as a landscape or a sunset, or quietly reading a book, when all of a sudden someone comes alive in your heart and thoughts? This is an opportunity for you to use a divine touch to pray for them, call them on the phone, minister to them, or some other way envelop them with love. The other side of that coin is suddenly someone calls you or searches you out, and tells you they have been thinking of you, and thought they would call to see how you are doing.

There is purpose in the pattern—a reason for the moment—and if it is not embraced, something important could be passed over. I try to embrace every experience. One weekend, Sharon and I traveled to Martinsville, VA, for a Saturday ministry meeting of a dear friend. Sunday morning, when we got up, I decided that rather than church, we were going to head back to Pennsylvania early. But because of the expectations of others who knew we were in town, we could not leave without letting the local pastor know; otherwise, someone would be offended.

When we got to the church, the pastor informed me that he was so excited to see us because a visiting minister was in town and he had made arrangements for us to have lunch with him. The man was Arthur Burt, from Wales. Arthur was Smith Wigglesworth's armor bearer. Arthur had traveled with Smith during his time of ministry in Europe. Our plans suddenly changed, and we weren't going anywhere but to church. God had spoken to Pastor David Hundley of Martinsville Christian Fellowship to make this luncheon. Soon after church, Sharon and I were sitting across from this visitor, a true blessing, and were able to enjoy a few hours of asking Arthur questions and hearing his answers from his first-hand experience of Wigglesworth's ministry. Why? I wanted to ask all of my questions because I had always been very curious about the life of Smith Wigglesworth. I often questioned my father about him, and told my father that he would have to prove that this man existed (by this time he had passed on). Instead, I sat with the man who had personally witnessed many of those who were raised from the dead, and was able to talk with him about the details of the books and writings about Smith Wigglesworth. Jesus interceded for me, through Pastor Hundley, and made a way for an unknown minister to meet this evangelist from Wales. This was intercession at its best. God saw that I knew the truth, He provided what I had asked Him for—being taught and led by the Spirit of God into the unknown (we had no idea of this happening)—to find this favor in Christ. To some it might have meant nothing, but to me and Sharon it was just the steppingstone we needed.

Intercession is not just for others but for ourselves, also. Jesus provides the perfect example. Take some time to read John chapter 17, where Jesus talks to the Father of His mission on earth. I want you to see that intercession is not just prayer; it is action, it is accountability, it is being Christ, not just talking about Him. I mentioned the names in chapter eight because no matter where I am, they are in my heart. We must also become sensitive to others who are touching lives we cannot. Sharon has those whom she can touch that I will never be able to, and when she mentions their names, I cannot take offense to them or even tell my wife that she does not have a place. If I expect her to be used of her Father, then I must let her be who she is and walk her walk out before her Father.

I could go on, but what is important is that you begin praying and asking the Father yourself to guide you by His Word and His Spirit into intercession. By the time this book went to editing, I was preparing to die, but God intervened with health. Today, as I sit and type this, I am walking in the best health of my life. I should be good for another thirty or forty years. What was intended to be a memoir will now be the beginning of more writings on intercession and prayer. I am full of joy and love to have been given this opportunity. I cannot encourage you enough to stop, drop, and pray. Learn to leave your agenda behind and let God begin to fill in the gaps of life. Find somebody who needs prayer and commit to that need. Stand in the gap and cry out for them. They don't even need to know; it is something that is between just you and the Lord.

Being part of a church has a bigger venue, and that is being part of the Kingdom of God. I say that if you serve in the Kingdom, you will fulfill your purpose in the church. Seek first the Kingdom of God, and all these things will be added unto you (Mt. 6:33). Go in peace. Thank you for spending this time with me. Look us up at www.needtopray.org. And as always, have a blessed journey in Jesus.

Let me close with a blessing: *Be healed. Be whole. Live well and prosper.*

If you would like Brian to pray for you or are interested in taking your prayer life to the next level, reach out at any of the following places.

Website: www.needtopray.org
Email: brian@needtopray.org
Facebook: Brian Kisner Outreach

Printed in Great Britain
by Amazon

75598366R00047